CHURCH
SERVICE
PRODUCTION

FULFILLING THE
GREAT COMMISSION

PAUL MANCUSO

Prominence Publishing
www.prominencepublishing.com

The author can be reached as follows:
Churchserviceproduction.com

Church Service Production/Paul Mancuso. -- 1st ed.

ISBN: 978-1-988925-97-4

To my wife Misty, my oldest son Landon,
and my youngest Greyson.
Serving in Service Production with you all
is the most fulfilling part of my life.

To my mom Trish Mancuso and my late Father,
Vincent A. Mancuso Jr. who both instilled in me
the love for church and service production.

To anyone who has struggled in
ministry at one time or another.

Special Thanks

(In No Particular Order)

*Pastor Jeff Ables , Pastor Jacob Aranza, Pastor Jay Miller,
and Pastor Don Norman thank you all for pastoring me and
showing me how to be a father, husband, leader, and friend.*

*To Shawn Marcell, Matt Lynch, and Tandi Begnaud
thank you for encouraging me, pushing me, and holding
me accountable to get this book completed.*

*To Pastor Marty Hoey, Pastor Frank Fowler,
and Pastor Mike Linney for giving me the opportunity
to serve in children's ministry when I was a child
and giving me the platform to grow my skills.*

*To Aaron Broussard, Jimmy Benoit, and the late
Rhian Quebedeaux. We have spent countless hours
working in churches together, thank you for
teaching me and working with me.*

*Thank you to my business partner Brandi Gwin and the best staff
in the world at Vital Integrators. I could not do what I do without
each of you, and I am eternally grateful.*

*To all worship leaders, pastors, service production personnel, and
volunteers that I have had the privilege of working with and
knowing. You all have been the inspiration for this book.*

TABLE OF CONTENTS

CHAPTER 1

CONNECTING THE *WHY* TO THE *WHAT*

WHY?

It is the foundation of understanding and often one of the first questions we learn to ask as children. It is one of the most basic questions that you can ask to gain an understanding of any subject. At its core, it is one of the smaller words and as a question, it is the simplest question you can ask. Sometimes the simplest questions are the most important.

You may ask yourself, "What makes you qualified to write a book on church service production?" To answer the *what*, we must answer the *why*. I could tell you stories of all the positions I have worked at as a volunteer, or been paid as a contractor, system designer, or installer, but the truth of the matter is that I am not qualified. Many other people out there are more qualified than I am to provide advice and direction. What I can tell you is the *why* behind it. I have seen almost every side of church service production—the good, the bad, and the downright ugly.

I have seen volunteers cry out of frustration and leave churches over misunderstandings, and Pastors that care about excellence but have financial constraints that limit those desires. I know the frustration of volunteers not showing up, never feeling like you have enough time to execute the vision of your leadership, not being appreciated when things go well, and being criticized when mistakes happen.

This all leads me to why I wrote the book and not what makes me qualified. If I can help one person, volunteer, paid staff, Pastor, or professional, it was all worth it. At the heart of service production, you have to start with the *why*. If you are like me, you enjoy technology and enjoy being behind the scenes. We help connect the *why* to the *what*. We use our gifts and talents to use tools (the *what*) to help reach people (the *why*).

THE *WHY*: THE GREAT COMMISSION

In Matthew 28:16-20, Jesus left us with what is known as The Great Commission[16].

Then the eleven disciples went to Galilee, to the
mountain where Jesus had told them to go.[17]
When they saw him, they worshiped him; but some
doubted.[18] *Then Jesus came to them and said, "All*
authority in heaven and on earth has been given to
me.[19] *Therefore go and make disciples of all nations,*
baptizing them in the name of the Father and of the
Son and of the Holy Spirit,[20] *and teaching them to*
obey everything I have commanded you.
And surely, I am with you always,
to the very end of the age."

This passage of scripture must be the core belief at the heart of church service production. One of the Pastors I served under every Sunday morning, would remind the team that you never know whose last service this will be. You cannot lose sight of this no matter what role you play on your team or in leading your team. It is about people. Fulfilling The Great Commission is at the heart of everything your hands find to do. Too often, it is easy to put a greater emphasis on those that are on stage over the ones that are behind the scenes.

Just about every church I have worked with or observed has had challenges between what I would call the creatives and the integrators. The creatives are usually your worship team members, graphic designers, stage designers, and worship leaders. The integrators are the people that execute the vision of the creatives. Most of the time the integrators are perfectionists and thrive on doing an excellent job. This can be incredibly frustrating when a worship leader (or creative) schedules six singers for a worship set, and your sound engineer (or integrator) knows you only have the equipment to handle four singers. The creative desires to perform at a level of excellence but is not typically concerned with the details.

An integrator desires to please the team and wants to accommodate but is unable to do so because of equipment limitations. You can point to poor communication between those two individuals, but it can also be a limitation or lack of communication between the worship leader and the budget office. When these things come up, it is easy to point at the *what* each person involved did instead of looking at the *why*. In church service production, your *why* should be considered your vision and your goal. Why do you do what you do? If everyone involved starts with that question defined for them, it makes the *what* a lot less important.

My dad told me many times growing up, "it's not what you say but how you say it." I would modify that just a little to say, it's not **what** you do but **why** you do it. You might lead worship, run sound, run a camera, or play the guitar. They are all different tools, but all have a common *why*.

THE *WHAT*: CHANGING THE METHOD, NOT THE MESSAGE

I was born on an October Sunday in 1982 in Morgan City, LA. George Harden was the Pastor of an Assemblies of God church, and my dad was the volunteer sound engineer. My mom was a Sunday school teacher and went into labor during Sunday school. To say my parents were committed volunteers is an understatement. I grew up alongside my parents at any church we attended and somehow or another we always ended up serving behind the scenes. My dad's love for ministry and media was passed on to me and I have spent most of my life involved in churches and ministries in some capacity. It is fun to watch the next generation as my children follow in those footsteps getting involved in service production.

While the *what* may change from generation to generation, the *why* does not change. The equipment was different when my dad was volunteering—they recorded services on cassette tapes. It was even different when I was involved. Now, my children live in a world where they do not even know what an iPod is. They assume all phones have been smartphones. The *what* has changed drastically through the years, but it is interesting to see that even through multi-generations, the *why* (or the goal) has remained constant.

Let us go back even further to when Jesus spoke those words in Galilee over 2000 years ago when he preached the Sermon on the Mount. Think about how powerful it would be to be able to watch that event! Despite the difficulty in understanding the dialect, it would undoubtedly be moving to experience that historical event. Unfortunately, technology did not exist to have any recording other than the words found in the Bible.

We currently live in a world where we can digitally preserve any event, at any time, for future generations to be able to watch. At no other point in history have we been able to capture events with the clarity, preservation, and instantaneous communication, that we can today. Technology is changing so rapidly, and the church is now able to reach people and preserve the message for generations to come.

Churches need to embrace technology trends and use them as a tool to accomplish the *why*. It can be tough to balance the desire to embrace technology and also maintain a sense of tradition. Through the recent Covid-19 pandemic, churches around the world were forced to embrace technology, as larger gatherings were often canceled or restricted. An entire global shift happened almost overnight, with churches embracing technology. Even the more traditional churches began to stream services and focus on reaching an audience they would have never been able to reach before. When churches were not able to meet, they turned to technology.

Suddenly, an emphasis on church service production was prioritized. It opened many people's eyes that may have been hesitant to embrace change. At the heart of it all, the *what* no longer mattered as much as the *why*. It is sometimes easy to be blinded by tradition or the way things have always been, but I believe as a member of your production team in any capacity, you have to always keep the why at the core of what you do.

If the why is your focus—the equipment, the building, the technology, the volume, the songs, or any distractions will no longer matter. They all become tools to fulfill the goal. If you think of technology as another tool, then you gain a better understanding that the what (or the tool) should not be your focus.

My *why* for this book is simple. I hope to impart some of the knowledge I have gained from the thousands of hours I have spent serving numerous Pastors and churches to help you find your own *why*.

One of the most memorable sermons I have ever heard was preached in the mid-1990's and I can almost repeat it word for word. Rev. Buddy Bell has a ministry and teaches on the Ministry of Helps, where he primarily focused on nursery workers, ushers, greeters and the like. His analogy of the body of Christ being like a carburetor is true. I could never do justice to how he told the story, but he explains that all the parts and pieces of a carburetor have to be put in place, fine-tuned, and operate together in order to get the full potential and full power out of the engine.

I would say that church service production is the carburetor of the church weekend experience. It is a central and integral piece of the service that has many moving parts that all have to work together simultaneously to reach its full potential. You can have a service without a production team, but how effective will it be? How effective will the preacher be able to preach, if no one can hear him? How effective would worship be if they had no lighting? How many more people can be reached with cameras streaming online?

Your job on the production team is to eliminate distractions for the people on stage by executing your job to the best of your ability. Your worship team and communicators in a service should be able to focus on worship and communication without distractions. You may think you are just in charge of putting lyrics to the song on the screen for the congregation, but you are also helping your worship team lead the congregation by leading them. You are helping your Pastor convey his sermon effectively by giving him visual notes and helping people in the audience take notes. You are never "just performing a job." You are utilizing the gifts and talents given to you by God to help reach people by eliminating distractions for your team and congregation. The fewer distractions your stage team has, the better job they can do. You do what you are good at, so they can do what they are good at.

All the parts must work together, and it starts with everyone understanding the *why*.

~ KEY TAKEAWAY ~

Define Your Why!

CHAPTER 2

IT'S NOT ABOUT YOU

Webster's dictionary defines ego as a person's sense of self-esteem or self-importance. Ego is a characteristic that can be both a blessing and a curse at times. I have never met a good production team member that did not have at least a bit of an ego. Just like other character issues, ego, when managed, is not all bad. I think we have been conditioned to think that having an ego is a totally bad thing. Yes, it makes people hard to deal with if they are not self-aware of that blind spot, but ego is also often confused with confidence.

Being confident in what you do and having the confidence of your leadership team to execute directives and make decisions on the fly, is a valuable and crucial part of church service production. When it comes to church service production, I would define ego as being more concerned about your opinion being validated or thinking your opinion is the most important in the room. This is a very dangerous mindset and can be cancer to a production team. Confidence, on the other hand, is knowing your self-importance or having confidence in your abilities paired with being humble.

MY IDEAL FORMULA WOULD BE EGO + HUMILITY + EMOTIONAL INTELLIGENCE = CONFIDENCE.

You need to be confident but not egotistical. It is hard to run any position on a production team without confidence. You need to be able to make decisions quickly (right or wrong) and be confident in your ability. Every good ensemble or team that has been put together has to be confident and not egotistical.

In professional sports, a team is made up of many players who execute different positions. They must be confident in themselves but also in their teammates. A quarterback must be confident when he throws the ball and have confidence his receiver will make the catch. The same can be said about the receiver. If he is only confident in his own ability and not confident in his quarterback, they will not be as successful.

Ego is wanting it to be about you. Confidence is wanting it to be about the vision. Confidence is understanding the *why* is more important than you. As a production team, you need to be confident in your ability and the ability of all your team members to work together to accomplish the ultimate goal—which is fulfilling the vision of the Pastor and leadership team.

VISION

When you sign up to serve on the production team, you are joining a very critical part of a weekend experience. Some Pastors are very involved in the production, and some are very hands-off. In either case, it is your job as a part of the team to execute the plays that your coach (Pastor) has designed. You are serving him to help fulfill the vision that God has given him for the church and the congregation. This is a very important and key understanding you must have.

Aside from defining the *why* as we discussed in Chapter 1, you need to align your vision with the vision of your Pastor. This sometimes means you disagree with the direction or disagree with a decision. Disagreement is healthy, disrespect is not. Going into each service knowing the common goal you are trying to achieve and the overall vision of your Pastor, will help you deal with disagreement in a respectful way. We will talk more about the intricacies of developing the trust of your Pastor and team in a later chapter but for now, let's focus on how to align your vision.

The *why* is not necessarily the same as the vision. The *why* is ultimately reaching people. The vision and/or the method are typically communicated by the Lead Pastor or leadership team. The vision could range from anything like specific lighting preferences, color preferences, audio levels, video ideas, or what type of microphone the speaker wants to wear.

Let me give you a practical example of how you can have a servant's heart and accomplish the vision of the Pastor. I was an audio engineer for a larger church in my area who would bring in many guest speakers throughout the year. The organization placed a huge emphasis on honoring those guests. Practically, how did that culture of honor make its way to the sound booth? How was the production team able to fulfill that culture or vision of the leadership team? Simply, we were prepared for every guest speaker. This meant talking to the guest before the service and asking them which microphone they preferred. We typically had three on hand to handle whatever preference they had.

We would offer a dual-ear headset, a single-ear headset, or a handheld. Why was this important? It was a demonstration of caring to make the speaker most comfortable. What would make them least distracted to deliver their message to the congregation? The culture of honor was emphasized in every team and the production team was no exception. Not only were we able to honor the wishes and vision of the Senior Pastor, but we also removed those distractions from the speaker as well. This is a culture you must work at building and creating for your team.

Volunteers are many times easier to deal with than those of us who do production in the secular market, professionally. It is sometimes hard to let our professional preference take a back seat to the vision that the Pastor wants. Our preference may be to put the speakers on a headset because it is easier to manage audio fluctuations. Maybe the speaker is more comfortable with a handheld but does not control the microphone well. It will take more work for you to manage the volume for the whole service in that case, but you are eliminating distractions from the one delivering the message. This is such a key part of understanding the basis for church service production.

Yes, you are valuable with your professional opinion and you may be right about the mic in the story above, but the ultimate goal is not your professional opinion— it is reaching people. I am not suggesting you do anything that would damage equipment or do something unsafe with rigging. If you are a professional, there is a place and time to bring those things up, but deciding which microphone or dB level you run, is not a hill you need to die on.

LEARN AND EDUCATE

I have been involved in the church my entire life, and in church service production for more than half of my life. I believe that the things I learned by being involved in some of the best production teams in the world, helped mold my mindset and shape the principles that I still use to this day. I have broken those down into five core values or as I call them in our business—The VITAL Way.

VITAL stands for Vision, Integrity, Teamwork, Attitude, and Leadership.

These are essentially the internal operating principles that we require our staff to exhibit and I think they are key when developing a culture for your production team. I have modified some of the descriptions slightly to focus on different aspects of your production team.

VISION

For each service, project, task, or install, clearly think through all steps and anticipate challenges. Have a clear vision and understanding of the scope of the work and anticipate any challenges you may have for service. Always look for ways to improve yourself, your team, and your processes. Set, meet, and exceed goals both personally and as a team.

INTEGRITY

Be honest in everything. When a mistake is made, be quick to own it. Never mislead or withhold information from your leadership team, volunteers, or team members. Hold integrity in the highest regard, this is a pillar of our ministry and vision.

TEAMWORK

We value teamwork. Not only does this apply to your team but also to strategic teams that you may interact with such as ushers, greeters, worship team, etc. Always be thinking of ways to improve workflow for the team. In projects or service workflows, use the *three C's—Communicate, Clarify, and Confirm.*

Communicate also means do not be afraid to ask questions.

Clarify is a step to make sure you understood what is being asked of you and the opportunity to raise any concerns.

Confirm when you have completed your tasks effectively.

Being late, not clear in communication, and not updating team members on changes are all disrespectful to the rest of the team. The same applies when communicating through either written or verbal communication.

ATTITUDE

The three key characteristics of volunteering in church service production that make up our definition of attitude is to be *Hungry, Humble, and Smart.* If you have not heard of the book, *The Ideal Team Player* by Patrick Lencioni, I highly recommend it. It breaks down the best parts of finding the right people on your team and starts with finding people who are *Hungry, Humble, and Smart.*

Be hungry in your quest for knowledge and put passion into your work. Be humble when mistakes are made or when receiving corrections or critiques. Be smart in not only expanding your knowledge, but also knowing when to say things and when not to, when to escalate issues, and when to ask for help. Remember, it's not what you say, but how you say it. We must be as polite as possible but also understand the demands and stress in the moment when in a production environment. Do not take offense if someone gives you constructive criticism while you are doing your job. Understand that it is for a reason and if needed, ask for clarification later.

LEADERSHIP

We believe everyone is a leader. We value ideas, opinions, and input from every team member. We want to hear what we can do to improve as a team. We realize everyone on the team has a different perspective and sometimes that perspective may be the best solution. You are leading either a new volunteer, helping fulfill the vision of the Pastor, or leading yourself by participating in personal growth. We will always be learning, leading, and growing both personally and as a team. We also know that our job is to put our leadership and Pastor's vision above our own while working towards the common goal of reaching people.

CULTURE

Your production team is only going to be as good as the culture you grow and cultivate. If your team is stagnant and not growing, try to evaluate why. Your team needs to understand the *why*, the vision, and the operating principles to create that team atmosphere and cohesion that is so important. Everyone on your team should be replicating the knowledge they have to other people on the team.

Your job as a leader is to identify your team's strengths and weaknesses and make sure you have everyone in the right seat on the bus. Sometimes you have to fill spots on the team with any warm body—especially if you are a smaller church or expanding your production with video or online streaming in a short window of time. To avoid burnout, make sure your team is passionate about the area they are working in. If you know it's not a long-term fit, identify what they are passionate about.

It's been said, "Find a job you love doing and you will never work a day in your life." The same is said about church service production. If you are passionate about it and love it, you will do that job with excellence and be great at it. If it's boring to you or you are just filling a role because you were asked, you likely will not serve long and experience burnout easily. If you are a volunteer and feel that way, talk to your leader to find an area that you *are* passionate about. If you are already serving in your desired role, identify people that are passionate about what *you are* and recruit them to serve with you. If you are a leader and have not evaluated your team, try to connect with them and work on identifying any areas that can be improved or positions that need to be changed.

~ KEY TAKEAWAY ~
Teach Your Vision, Culture, and Share Your Knowledge.

CHAPTER 3

I NEED VOLUNTEERS

When speaking with church leaders about church service production, there seem to be two consistent obstacles: a) we have no budget, or b) we have no volunteers. We will discuss budgets in a later chapter, but the volunteer aspect of church service production is a hard one and it often gets harder as you grow and scale. It is typically not a problem that ever goes away completely though the challenges change with growth and scale. You begin to see different issues arise and how you manage them is important to maintaining a cohesive team.

If you follow the steps in the last two chapters, by now your core team should have a clear understanding of the *why*, as well as defined roles and operating principles that are clearly communicated. Laying the foundation early with your team, makes recruiting new volunteers and raising up leaders that can train and lead based on your core values, a much easier process.

The unique, as well as challenging, part of service production is that you have so many personality types on the team. Navigating this is difficult to do especially when you only see each other once a week or less, if you are privileged to have a larger production team.

Unlike with a worship team, where it is most likely they are creatives; on a production team, you will have people with many different personality types and skill sets that can be hard to manage. I find that most people are not as fulfilled by just "filling a seat." They want to be part of the process and part of something bigger. If you can impart to them the importance of the role they play that it is such an integral part of the ministry that takes place in a service, it will help them feel a sense of responsibility and fulfillment.

Understanding the *why* is such an important part of the volunteer team. Aside from the personal connection you have with the team, communicating is the number one way to help define your culture. If you are having trouble recruiting or keeping volunteers, communicating the vision is likely an area you can improve upon. I know it is very cliché, but having the right foundation for your team is the most important thing you can do to solidify your culture and develop consistency between volunteers.

Knowing Your Team

Service production is easy with the right team; finding, keeping, and growing that team is difficult. The best word that I can give you as a leader or a volunteer, is *intentional*. As a volunteer, you need to be very *intentional* in what you want to learn and how you want to grow. You need to be intentional in seeking out relationships with other volunteers, people that you can invest in, and your leadership team. If you oversee service production, it's very easy to get lost in the process of executing at a high level and forget about the people in the process.

Your volunteers are also a part of those people you are trying to reach, and they should be elevated and honored for the service they perform. You can't develop a real relationship with them by only working together for a few hours on a Sunday. You have to be intentional about developing that relationship outside of the booth. I highly recommend reading *The 5 Levels of Leadership* by John Maxwell, as you are learning or improving your leadership skills when it comes to your production team.

I firmly believe that without these connections and touches outside of the booth on Sunday, you will always struggle with leading your team. Using a sports analogy, the baseball team does not just meet on game day. They get together and practice during the week, and then work together to execute at a high level on game day. Your team is not going to win every week. Your volunteers are going to make mistakes and you will have better days than others. You will need to work with your Pastors and staff to help define and set expectations—especially if you are in the early stages of building a team or implementing major growth initiatives such as online streaming or major equipment replacements.

SETTING EXPECTATIONS

I see this happen over and over and it pains me to read about how burnt out people get as volunteers when it comes to church service production. Almost every week I read a Facebook post about someone ready to quit and leave a church or stop volunteering because they are not being heard or they are frustrated with the unrealistic deadlines or expectations. I know I reference foundations and core values a lot, but this is so key in building a quality team and it is often overlooked or never addressed. If you are over service production, many times you get good at jumping off the cliff and building the plane on the way down. You can pull off small miracles each week but have little time to feel like you are growing and building a healthy team.

You as the leader, need to be able to communicate this with your leadership team and Pastors. As you grow this team, you should want excellence, but not perfection. Some Pastors can be very hard to keep on schedule and they do not fully understand the time constraints and the technical challenges created by their last-minute changes. It is important to have a very open dialog with those involved in a weekend experience and make sure everyone understands the expectations.

For instance, if you pay professionals to show up and run your production team and all positions are staffed by industry professionals, your expectation for excellence will be much higher. The problems I often see, occur when the lead staff (who often do not understand the intricacies of production), set that same expectation on volunteers. Without properly setting those expectations, you play the dangerous game of burnout or volunteers being offended. As the leader, you may also feel like a failure because of your Pastor's disappointment. All of those feelings and emotions can be valid and warranted, but they can also be avoided if communication is made ahead of time and expectations are properly set.

There is a fine line between excellence being a core value and a volunteer feeling like they can never measure up. It's all in how you define expectations and build that relationship. If you know you have a new person running lighting or sound, you should prepare the staff for possible mistakes. It is all part of the learning process. So much of what is done during a service is so hard to train for until it happens and until your team gets hands-on time doing the job. The added pressure of a new volunteer to be able to perform mistake-free because expectations were not properly set can turn people off to even wanting to volunteer.

Remember, most of the people who volunteer in these positions, enjoy being behind the scenes. They typically do not like the spotlight and really don't like it when something goes wrong. The volunteer sound engineer may never be noticed for 51 weeks out of the year, but the one weekend he makes a mistake and the whole congregation is looking at him, can crush his spirit if handled wrong. If you are the leader, you need to be responsible for setting those expectations for your team and the staff of the church.

You also need to have a good way to measure success. Have a few goals for each position that are clear and precise and not general. It is more helpful to the person volunteering to know specifically what a win looks like. If you have a very vague win of, "We didn't have any mistakes," then even one single mistake means it was a failure. Example wins for your presentation volunteer may look something like this:

1. Song notes were entered correctly
2. Worship slides were accurate and advanced properly
3. Video transitions were executed correctly
4. Speaker's notes and scripture references were accurate
5. What could have been better?

It is important that you define these for each role. It helps you train and coach the person and helps them feel like it was still a win even if something did not go as planned. Using the above example, if a video transition did not cue correctly, they still nailed 90% of the job. Having a very vague gauge is dangerous because it can lead to a drop in morale on your team if it makes them feel like the entire thing was a failure.

It is also important to celebrate the wins and not focus as much on what went wrong. Praise your team for what they do right each week. End every position's win sheet with what could have been better? It puts the question to them to identify something to work on. As a culture, this will help develop a spirit of excellence in what they do.

THE TECHNICAL DEBRIEF

I think it is important to engrain in your culture that nothing is ever perfect. You are not seeking perfection, but excellence. The way you model this is to ask everyone on your team what could have been better? It allows a posture for them to be open about what went wrong and is a culture of accountability, not condemnation. As a leader, you should start each meeting by saying an area that you know *you* could improve on or owning a mistake that *you* made.

As the leader, it is also super important to cover the Pastor and staff if they are frustrated and not pass that on to your team. Equally important is having the back of your volunteers to the leadership team. Do not take any criticism from the leadership team back to your volunteers. It should always be presented in a way to improve and be a collective collaboration. Be open to your team's advice and critiques on your leadership style and allow them to be open about each other.

It is important to navigate this away from personal opinion and make sure it is defined by a win. For instance, you may have three opinions on your team about what background should have been used on the screen for a song. If that is not defined as one of the wins for that area, this should be avoided.

Service production is one of the most subjective areas of ministry and everyone seems to have an opinion. Of course, each one feels that their opinion is correct. Try and avoid that in a group setting and address that one-on-one, if needed. It is important to have a debrief meeting with your team and I would suggest doing it after every service. If necessary, include the worship leader in those meetings in case they need to make adjustments. This also gives them a place of honor and respect on your team as service production is largely part of serving the needs of the band and worship team.

Building this cohesive group is very important as your church grows and as the production and worship teams grow. Your teams need to start looking like one unit instead of two different ministries trying to minister at the same time.

THE TWO-HEADED MONSTER

I will not say every church, but almost every church I have had the opportunity to work with seems to have a conflict at one point or another between the technical

team and the worship team. This is generally mani-
fested by either team not recognizing the *why* in the
moment or letting ego be the dominant character trait
over confidence.

If your worship team and tech team are not on the
same page, you have a two-headed monster than will
never be tamed. Many of the suggestions and practices
in this book are to help set core values and expectations
between your teams to enable you to avoid that. While
all of that is a good start, you cannot leave out team
building. If the only interaction your worship team has
with the production team is at a service time, you are
inevitably setting yourself up for failure.

Many churches of all denominations have small groups
in one form or another. Instead of encouraging your
volunteers to join small groups offered by the church, I
think it is more effective to use your team as your small
group. Of course, this can be modified if your church is
offering specific sessions like finance or children's
groups, etc. But as a general rule, having a small group
for your team will help cultivate the relationship outside of a service with your volunteers. It gives them the
ability to build *quality* relationships rather than just
working relationships on a Sunday morning.

As a leader, this also solidifies your role as a spiritual leader and not just a producer or service coordinator doing his or her job.

I also suggest and encourage you to bring in your Lead Pastor, Worship Pastor, and other leaders to help cultivate those relationships with them as well. I would advise Pastors to come and speak life, vision, and praise to the team. If they have criticism, however, it should go through the service production leader, and never from the Pastors directly to the volunteers.

Many people want to know that the Pastor noticed the job they did or appreciate them for the role they play on Sundays. It is often too busy for those conversations to be had on a service day. But, it helps bring personal human interaction with the teams. To me, this is one of the largest pieces left out of many production teams no matter the size of the church. With a very small church, it may seem awkward or unnecessary. It is. But if your intention is to grow, it gives you a great foundation to build from. If you are a super large organization, it is easy to say, "that is why my Pastor hired someone to manage production." You cannot outsource that role to your team. What they do and what they are helping you to accomplish as a Pastor, is far too important for you not to take a few hours out of your month to invest back in them.

I see so many churches skip this critical step and wonder why they are unable to grow the production team. Invest in what you want a return from. I cannot stress enough how important this part of the puzzle is. It is also encouraged to have the worship team and the production team get together at least once a month. This allows for individuals to build relationships with each other, instead of just being acquainted because they both serve at the same service.

Your role as a leader is to create the connection points to allow relationships to grow. Remember the *why* is to reach people. You need to reach the people in your circle of influence, too. Do not overlook the people entrusted to you that serve with you. They are people with problems, challenges, prayer requests, and praise reports just like everyone else who comes on Sunday.

Be mindful of how often they are working. If you are small and have the same crew working just about all services, the small group is even more critical. Be aware, be available, and be intentional.

~ KEY TAKEAWAY ~
Be Intentional and Set Expectations.

CHAPTER 4

HE WHO HAS EARS
LET HIM HEAR

I remember as a little boy growing up in church, I was mesmerized by anything to do with service production or technology. At the time that I really became interested, my dad was working over the media department and in charge of editing the television show and all the responsibilities that go along with that. I remember many nights being up at the church with him while he edited, and I would roam the campus of the church and somehow always end up drawn to the audio console. I really did not know what the equipment was, though it always seemed to call my name. Although I enjoyed video, my passion and my natural desire has always been audio.

I was fortunate enough to attend a church that was not afraid to allow kids to serve and put their hands on something at a young age. Over 25 years later, it was because of the investment in me and the freedom to allow a 10-year-old kid to pursue his passion that I am now able to do that for a living in my own business. Those years that I volunteered set a foundation for me to be mentored and trained, and give me the knowledge and experience that I have today.

I remember that when I was maybe 11 or 12 years old, our church had a kid's ministry that would meet on Sunday nights. I was never really one to connect and be social, but put me behind the audio console and I was right at home. I could talk about audio for hours. One of these nights, however, I was running sound for the service, and someone knocked a full can of soda onto the soundboard causing it to short out and burn up. I will never forget that feeling. Even though I was not the one who had knocked it over, I still felt responsible because I was running the console at the time.

I remember being so devastated that I allowed that to happen and replayed the event in my head 1000 times. I distinctly remember feeling like I would never get to serve doing what I loved because of this. As a 12-year-old who had no concept of money, I was thinking this console was worth $100,000! In reality, it was probably worth about 1% of that. But that moment instilled two things that have never left me to this day. If I am around any sound booth at all—even 25 years later—and I see an open drink, you can bet I am going to speak up about it. People that have an unhealthy habit of having drinks near electronics have clearly never had one dumped on an audio console.

The second lesson that I learned that day was that I never wanted to stop doing what I loved. The fear of not getting to do what I enjoyed so much, and was so passionate about, and felt that I did well, made me realize how much I enjoyed sound. I cannot put into words the indescribable feeling of stepping up to the sound console, pushing that master fader up, feeling the power of the subs hit you in the chest as the band starts the song with a deep kick drum. As the song progresses and you are moving through the console hitting guitar solos and making the band sound good... there is no feeling like that in the world. The only thing that can top that is when the show is over, and you turn off the system and sit back to realize that it was a near-perfect show. I hit all my cues, the sound was awesome, and the crowd responded. For an audio guy, THAT'S his big win.

Nothing can explain that feeling and 25 years later, I still feel that in my bones for every note that is played, every lyric that is sung, and every crowd reaction. I had that feeling from the first time I ran sound until last week when I was running sound as a 38-year-old man. This chapter is not going to be a "how-to" chapter as much as it will be about guardrails. I will give you some general guidelines and parameters to use to help you build a mix and experience that feeling for yourself.

For me, that feeling cannot be replicated or replaced by anything. It is a high that I can only imagine a football player feels when scoring a touchdown or making the game-winning tackle. I never played sports as a kid as I was homeschooled, and my passion and extracurricular activities revolved mostly around church and service production specifically. There is a running joke in my circle of friends that helps articulate what I mean.

For the most part, audio engineers either love it or hate it. They usually have no in-between. While my dad was over video growing up, Jimmy Benoit was the audio engineer. He and his wife Brenda had a studio at the church and if I worked cameras for my dad on a Sunday morning, I would get off camera and go sit and watch in the audio booth. I am sure the annoying 10-year-old kid asked a thousand questions too many, but no one ever crushed my spirit or got frustrated.

To this day, Jimmy is still like a father figure to me—even more now that my dad has passed on. Jimmy owned a production company that was hired to do the district Assemblies of God Youth Convention each year and I would go with him and work the event. It was on one of those trips that I made a comment that to this day, is still a running joke among our group of friends. We were discussing sound and I said, "I just love sound." I absolutely meant what I said in the moment, but it has since been a joke every time something didn't go right or there was a conflict someone would inevitably look at me and say, "I just love sound" in a sarcastic condescending tone.

Going back to culture for a minute, the church we were at had a culture to embrace youth. In fact, the kid's program I was running sound for when the drink was spilled was called New Life and the scripture, they would always recite to us was 1 Timothy 4:12 which I still remember today, it states:

"Don't let anyone look down on you because you are young, but set an example for the believers in speech, in conduct, in love, in faith, and in purity."
1 Timothy 4:12

This was modeled in the DNA and the culture of the church and was demonstrated by the willingness to teach me, allow me to make mistakes, but ultimately allow me to serve and develop the talent that was given to me. Pastor Marty Hoey gave me the opportunity when I was 10 years old to serve by running sound every week in kids church. Since he was so willing to allow kids to live out this scripture, I credit much of my passion to him for allowing to develop those skills in a safe environment.

So, I still say, "I just love sound." It's true though. If you are a sound engineer at heart, you probably love it. Yes, it can be incredibly frustrating and yes, it is hard to manage tension in the moment but deep down, you are always looking for that win, that feeling you get when you feel the power coming from those speakers. It's hard to not be passionate about something you love.

IT'S NOT THE EQUIPMENT

So many times, I hear stories from audio engineers that feel defeated. I will hear things like, "My Pastor visited this conference and wants our sound to be like that." Or, "You need to call this church and see what they are doing to make it sound so good." Remember earlier we talked about setting expectations? Well, this is a good example of that. Often, people will compare the result, the product, with the end result of someone else. The method, equipment, budget, and all the ways of how they got there are not the same. I see this happen over and over again where you start comparing yourself or the equipment you have with large churches with million-dollar systems and get discouraged about why things are not improving.

I could write an entire book on this subject, but I will try to summarize it this way. You have heard the phrase compare apples to apples, oranges to oranges, etc. My advice is very simple. If you are just starting out or want to find ways to improve, stop comparing yourself to large churches with big budgets—unless you have a large church and a big budget. The better option is to find a church you respect that is doing it well, and emulate them. The key is to find one with a similar demographic, similar budget, and similar vision. When you sit and compare notes with them, at least it is attainable, and you have commonality in your plans.

Part of your job as an audio engineer is to be able to make your system sound as good as you possibly can. Produce a product that is the best product you can produce with the budget you have. If you get really good as an engineer, you should be able to use almost any system and get a good sounding mix. Yes, A LOT of variables and things go into what I am saying. The room, acoustics, system power, EQ, consoles, all play a part in the overall feel of the system but do not excuse humble beginnings or budget constraints as an excuse to not make yourself better. It's easy to say, "well if I had the budget, they had I could make it sound that way." I will say it like this, not a single mega-church began as a mega-church. Not a single church with a million-dollar budget for audio started there.

Use what you have to the best of your ability. Be a good steward of what you have been given and refine your skills, get better, learn as much as possible on the small system, and grow with what you have. I have run sound on a half-million-dollar rig and a few weeks ago I ran a 2-input console with an iPod and a microphone. Do you know what both of those systems had in common? They both gave me the same feeling when the show was over. Running a 96-channel digital console gives me the same feeling as that 2-channel console. I will still say to this day, "I Just Love Sound!"

OK, WELL MAYBE IT IS SOME OF THE EQUIPMENT

As an audio engineer, the rest of this chapter will focus on some general principles, but the main principle you need to start with, is it's not about the equipment. That is more of the foundation we need to lay before we go forward because I do not want anyone to use the equipment they have as an excuse to not get better.

You should always look for ways to improve even if you have an adequate system and substantial budget. I want to address some mistakes I see churches make and hopefully help you if you are currently in one of the following scenarios.

SMALL CHURCH, SMALL BUDGET

If you are not a small church with a small budget, you probably know someone in ministry who is. What is a small budget to some, may not be a small budget to others. It's all about your perspective. When you are part of a smaller church, one of the biggest mistakes I see is using the scarce budget dollars on a project that you do not have the budget to do correctly or adequately.

One of the most common areas for this is wireless microphones or in-ear monitors. If you have not invested in in-ear monitors, it is usually the number one thing people want because it helps lower stage volume. I agree with both the reason, and the need. I also know that if you do not do this properly, your musicians are going to struggle, your leadership may think it was a bad investment, and it may not be an improvement overall.

Some things you just can't 'cheap-out' on. Anything wireless that is quality is usually not budget-friendly.

Being a good steward of the budget that you control, my suggestion is to not attempt to do in-ear monitors or wireless microphones, until you have the budget saved to do it correctly. Otherwise, it will be like throwing good money after bad, to fix problems that could have been avoided by getting the correct equipment in the first place. If you come across the right deal, it could also be a better option to buy higher quality wireless equipment from another church that is upgrading rather than buying something cheap.

Sometimes we try to fix the immediate problem as cheaply as possible but often it is important to have quality equipment. I would rather have a $100 SM58 wired microphone for all of my singers, than a cheap wireless system that will have to be replaced every year or that causes interference. It may be less convenient to live with the corded microphones, but in the long run, it is a much better option until you can do wireless correctly.

BUILDING PROJECTS

For churches that are in building projects, make sure you have a very frank conversation with your architect and builder about the expectations and needs in the space. I am bringing up building projects because this is something you can control. If you are not currently in a building project, these are some things to learn for a later date, when you do have a building to design.

If you build a building and the room is an echo chamber, it does not matter how much money you spend on a sound system, it will not sound good. I will say this as strongly as I can, *I would never build a building without having an acoustic designer involved in the project*. It is easy to get caught up in the design and aesthetics of the building and totally miss this crucial part. An acoustic designer will work with the contractor to make sure things in the building are designed to not interfere with your sound system. They will tell you how much treatment to put on the walls to cut down reverberation and where to install air handlers and AC units to not be heard in the worship space.

These things are extremely expensive to try and correct after the building is complete, so getting the infrastructure right is key. Part of that infrastructure is also the conduit runs for your AVL systems. You want to include those contractors in the process as early as possible to make sure power requirements and conduit runs are adequate to facilitate current needs as well as future growth. This can turn into a costly mistake if these things are overlooked. You can have the best sound system money can buy, but if you do not have adequate power or conduit runs to be able to get the wire to plug it in, or if the room is an echo chamber, you will never get the opportunity to build a great mix.

BUILDING A GREAT MIX

Building a great mix can be hard to imagine if you spend your time frustrated as a sound engineer. I am going to give you some very basic standard operating procedures. Sound, I would say, is the most subjective position in church service production. You can ask 10 different sound engineers their opinion on a mix and get 10 different opinions. Therefore, it is important to capture the vision of your Pastors and leadership and work on that each week. If you are new to this, find out what they did or did not like and try to adjust. If you are trying to improve and learn, the only way to get better is to build trust.

To start with, you must know the parameters and vision you are trying to accomplish. One of the biggest questions to discuss with your team is what target volume is acceptable? You do not want to be so loud that you are hurting people's ears, but do not want to be so low that the congregation has no energy. I would not focus as much on a dB number or reading. The number is not as important as knowing and feeling the response of the room.

KNOW THE ROOM AND YOUR SYSTEM

Before building a mix, you need to know the room nuances and equipment. Is everything in working order? Does the room have any hot spots? What does it sound like where the Pastor sits? Was the system properly tuned? These are questions you should know the answers to, before starting to mix.

Depending on what type of speaker you have and what throw angle they have will determine how loud it is upfront as opposed to where you may be mixing from in the back. It is important to know how the room sounds so you can adjust your mix accordingly. If you do not have the experience to run an analyzer in the room, I would suggest you have a professional come in and do that and tune your system to the room you are using. This will alleviate issues and help you have a solid foundation to start from.

You should not have to do this very often if you are not making major changes to the system or the building. I do recommend having it done at least once, if nothing more than learning the process and giving you peace of mind that your system is functioning properly and was professionally tuned. You also need to know and under-stand the limits of your system. If it is not properly powered or if the system is too small for the size of the room, that affects how loud you can run it as well. Getting all of that out of the way ahead of time is key to a good mix for service.

It's Showtime

The countdown is on the screen, you have 60 seconds, you unmute the band and your heart is racing as the countdown strikes one and the band hits the first note on the song and your job has just begun. Many opinions exist on sound and theory, but this is just a general rule of thumb to help you with some parameters to build off of. Audio is probably the hardest service production position to train someone on because it changes week to week, song to song, and it is so subjective on mix style.

If you are a musician and you struggle to get a good in-ear mix, I would recommend many of these same principles for how to get your ear mix to sound better. The foundation you start with is your drums and bass. Then bring in your acoustic guitar, electric, keys, tracks, etc. Build off the drums and bass and add things as needed. You will be mixing the entire song, so you really are not able to set a fader and forget it. Once you have the base of all of your instruments mixed well, then add your vocals on top of the mix. Having multiple singers can be tough to mix and you should always be ready to adjust them up or down depending on songs, parts, and being ready if they are very dynamic. Some of the details here change if you are mixing a separate mix for online, but this should give you a good foundation to start from.

With the introduction of digital consoles, we have so much more processing power at our disposal at a relatively lower cost. If you have already made the jump to a digital console understanding and utilizing the compressors, gates, reverb, and EQ built into the consoles is key to having a mediocre mix versus a great mix. These tools can be hard to set correctly so understanding your specific console and how to adjust settings quickly and on the fly is important to practice.

Sometimes people use compressors more as a volume control instead of catching peaks and they set it so high they do not have to mix. I discourage using it this way because it degrades the sound and makes for a lazy sound engineer. You should actively be mixing and engaged in every song while monitoring the tools at your disposal. Another common issue is people who are new to digital consoles sometimes get too caught up in what the EQ may look like on-screen vs what it actually sounds like. If it sounds good, it does not matter what it looks like. Mix with your ears, not your eyes.

FEEDBACK

I am not going to give you any tips and tricks on how to avoid feedback, on the contrary, you need feedback. Good communication is the foundation for a great production team and that starts with feedback from your leadership team. When the service is over, seek out your worship leader or Pastor and ask for feedback on how the service went. Ask them if they need anything or any adjustments that may be required between services if you have more than one service.

As audio engineers, we are conditioned to avoid feedback at all costs. Do not avoid the feedback of your leadership team, remember you are helping fulfill their vision and you should want to hear from them what they thought and how you can improve. This is the only type of feedback you should want to hear as an audio engineer.

As a Pastor or leader, it is also your responsibility to give feedback. Many times, we remember to give feedback when something needs to be adjusted, corrected, or when something didn't go as planned. It is equally important that you show appreciation and give recognition when things go right or when you have no real issues. This will allow your team to know you notice them when they are unnoticeable (no mistakes).

Remember, they are striving to serve you and have a heart to not disappoint the team. If they only hear from you when a mistake is made, that can be devastating to morale and lead to burnout. This is especially true if you have no problem confronting mistakes or changes. If someone is new to the team, it may be best to filter those comments through your team leader rather than the person who may have made a mistake. As important as it is for your team to seek out feedback, leaders need to learn to give feedback both good and bad as this helps cultivate a culture of honor on the team.

Honor as a culture is one of the key ingredients to an all-star team. As a leader, if you honor your volunteers, you are modeling how you want them to cultivate relationships both with you and the leadership team but also with the volunteers working with them as well. Honor is a key component of giving and receiving feedback and should be part of the culture you help develop on a weekly basis.

~ KEY TAKEAWAY ~

Love What You Do and Embrace Feedback!

CHAPTER 5

VIDEO PRODUCTION

Short of starting a new church and developing your production team from the ground up, starting a video team is probably one of the most difficult things to do, but also one of the easiest roles to train. The biggest obstacle you will encounter with a video ministry is simply the sheer number of volunteers you will need to do this effectively.

In this chapter, we will focus on the foundation of a basic video setup and define what each position is responsible for. We will dive deeper into live streaming later in this chapter, but for now we will focus on what you need to plan for to have an effective video team. The basic theme of this book is starting with the why behind what you are doing and defining that vision.

As with any other ministry or position, a video team is no different. My advice is to try to plan your vision 5-

10 years out, so you know how to phase in different projects over time. How you execute video is going to largely depend on what your overall vision is.

For example, if your goal is to one day have a live stream with a separate audio mixer and lower third graphics, some infrastructure should be put in place now instead of trying to add it later such as power requirements, audio splitter, or DANTE protocols and the like. If you are in a new building or reconstruction phase and eventually want to put an LED wall on your stage as a backdrop, providing power and conduit ahead of time during construction will save you time and money later. These decisions should be made with your Pastor and leadership team to capture the vision and goals that they want to accomplish.

Once you determine your vision, you need to assemble your team. Do not be discouraged if you do not have the equipment or personnel to fill all of these roles. This is hopefully a good foundation for you to get some insight to help train yourself or your team in any of these positions. I realize everyone has different budgets and equipment, but the hope is that you find value and have a plan to grow your equipment and team. If you are not in a place financially to have all of these things in place and you just have a single camera, focus on being the best camera operator you can be, so you are ready to train more volunteers as funds and your ministry grow.

TEAM MEMBERS

CAMERA OPERATORS

It goes without saying, you cannot have a video team without cameras and operators to run them. The great thing about camera operators is you can train almost anyone to be a quality camera operator provided you teach them some basic terms that can keep them within safe parameters.

When I took an interest in video production, the very first job I had was running camera. My dad was the director at the time, and he would tell me, "Protect the camera at all costs, always get the shot!" This became real to me one time when I was filming a kid's camp at the bowling alley that was a blacklight event. I was backing up to get the shot and tripped over something and fell straight back but caught the camera on my chest keeping it unharmed.

The camera is the single most important part of television production equipment. It is important that you understand the basic function and operation of the television camera. What the camera can do, and the capability and versatility of the camera operator directly determine all other TV production equipment and production techniques. As you become a seasoned camera operator or start training your team, have them think about the following:

- Decide composition for the beginning and end of the shot.
- Practice your movement until you can do it smoothly.
- Concentrate on shot composition.
- Is the foreground interesting?
- Is the background interesting?
- Is there empty space in the shot?
- Is 10% of the frame designated to headroom?
- Is the camera on eye level with the subject?

CAMERA HANDLING

The movement and positioning of a video camera is an art. It is essential to good video production that all camera movement is done as smoothly and artistically as possible. To accomplish this, a video camera operator must first be completely familiar with the six basic camera movements: panning; tilting; trucking; dollying; zooming; booming.

- PANNING – Can be defined as a movement of the camera in a horizontal plane. In other words, the camera swings left or right while the base or tripod of the camera remains stationary. A pan is used to illustrate to the viewer the relative size of an area, to follow the action from one location to another, and also to indicate the amount of distance between two subjects in a scene.

- TILTING – is a camera movement, which is executed, in a vertical plane. When tilting, the camera tripod again remains stationary while the camera is moved vertically either upward or downward. A tilt is used to obtain a lower or higher angle within a scene, to show the relative height of an object such as a shot down into a canyon.

- TRUCKING – Physically moving the camera left or right.

- DOLLYING – Physically moving the camera forward or backward.

- ZOOMING – Simply put, zoom is a continuous change of the focal length of the lens. Zoom can be accomplished through either mechanical or electrical means and is one of the most used camera movements in television production. Zoom allows you to move in close or back away from your subject without physically moving the camera.

- BOOMING – Raising or lowering the height of the camera.

GENERAL GUIDELINES FOR CAMERA OPERATORS

- Do not leave the camera pointed into the lights or any other bright object, this can damage the computer chips in cameras and create burn spots over time.

- Do not move the entire camera unit or otherwise take both hands off the pan handles without LOCKING the camera head down first and making sure that it is locked securely. If your tripods and heads are properly balanced, you can remove your hands while running the camera, but as a general rule, you should be ready for sudden movements or unexpected directions from your director. When leaving your station, ensure the cameras are in a locked position before leaving.

- Do not step on camera cables (or any other cables). They are made up of numerous fine wires and these wires could be easily broken. Newer cameras can also be run over fiber optic, which is fragile as well.

- If you must speak to the director during the actual production, do so very quietly so that you do not disturb anyone around you. Sometimes it can be hard to determine your volume if you have a dual-ear headset on, thus making it hard to tell how loud you are talking. It is also distracting to your production team if you leave the intercom mic on, especially during loud parts of a service like worship.

- Keep your eyes on the viewfinder. You should strive to always have a usable shot ready if the director should need it in a hurry. Making sure you are paying attention to your shot composition will help your director have confidence in your ability to anticipate the type of shot needed.

- Unless otherwise specified by the director, the eyes of the talent should be positioned on an imaginary horizontal line positioned one-third down from the top of the picture. Additionally, keep the talent's nose on an imaginary vertical line through the middle of the viewfinder. Also, you should lead the subject when following side-to-side movements, otherwise, it appears as if talent is "walking into a wall." When talent is reading from the pulpit, try to keep the pulpit just at the bottom of the screen, so the viewer can see the area where the talent is looking. It can look a bit weird if your Pastor is looking down and you do not see what he is looking at.

- All camera movements that are done while on-air, should be as subtle as possible. Otherwise, the viewers' attention is distracted from the program content. Your job is to be as distraction-free as possible. If you are running a handheld camera on stage or for crowd shots, it is even more important that you try to minimize movements to not distract those in a live service setting. I also recommend dark clothing for all your camera crew that will be in front of an audience.

- If you should have to move the entire camera unit (TRUCK, DOLLY, etc.) do so only after first locking down the head of the tripod. Only then would you move the unit, and then by the tripod legs, NOT the pan handles!

- Practice zooming, panning, and tilting before the start of the production. Adjust the pan and tilt friction knobs so that all camera movements will be smooth and even.

CAMERA SHADER

When you get to the point that you have multiple cameras, you may want to have a position called a camera shader. This person would be responsible for ensuring white balance, color correction, and iris settings maintain consistency between camera shots. If you have the budget, it is best to use a waveform monitor and vectorscope, especially if you will be broadcasting on a local television station. This will help keep your video within the parameters set for broadcast standards.

If you are not airing on television, you can get by without those pieces of equipment but still want to be as consistent as possible between camera shots. When making adjustments, try to make adjustments on the preview monitor and never on the live shot. Your goal in this position is to make sure all your cameras are as close to visually the same as possible. It is sometimes difficult if you have different brands of cameras or even different models, so this position is important to maintain consistency.

DIRECTOR

The video director is the person in charge of directing the camera operators, switching between them, recording/streaming, and instrumentals in the entire video process. This person is typically a good multitasker who has a high-capacity personality. This can vary from church to church, but generally, they are also responsible for any graphics that are put on the screen such as lower thirds for song lyrics or sermon notes. While they are not the ones running the actual presentation software, the switcher will usually have a downstream key function that overlays the graphics on top of the live video from the cameras. You will need to be able to communicate clearly and confidently to your team. If you have multiple volunteers that fill the role of director from time to time, you must standardize the camera operator's instructions, so it is consistent and does not cause confusion from week to week.

VIDEO PRODUCER

As your video team begins to grow, you may find it necessary to add a video producer over the whole team. This role would work closely with the front-of-house team to ensure communication is thorough and clear direction is given. This role is vitally important especially if your video equipment resides in a room outside of the auditorium or generally away from the front-of-house team.

Your role as a video producer is to coordinate between all positions and anticipate challenges, obstacles, and solutions before they become problems. Typically, this person would be in charge of making sure all aspects of the video ministry were working together and be available to help troubleshoot problems as they come up. During service, you would be overseeing your camera operators, shader, and director. It is helpful to have someone who can be following an order of service calling out what is coming next. This helps the flow of service and helps to eliminate miscommunication and has everyone hearing one voice for direction.

You may help with giving direction to the person shading cameras, help your director with camera shot composition, and provide general advice as things come up with the service. You are essentially the oil that is making the machine run smoothly. This role is vital to have in place before going live on the internet. If you have plans on streaming live, you will want to make sure you have a video producer that is capable and trained beforehand.

LIVE STREAMING

If you have already started or are thinking about doing live streaming, understand that it can be expensive to do it correctly but can be a great outreach tool as well. I remember one Sunday the church I was serving had a message on baptisms and at the end of the service, an invitation was made for anyone that wanted to be baptized to come forward. Over 100 people spontaneously came forward to get baptized and the line was so long they were still baptizing people when the next service started.

If you have ever thought that what you do is only behind the scenes, or that you go unnoticed—when you live stream, you open up your audience to people that would maybe never have stepped foot in a church. While baptisms were taking place during the second service that day, a family had been watching online, heard the invitation to be baptized, then drove to the church and got baptized that Sunday. The volunteers that were a part of the video team all had a hand in that family getting baptized. Every position in the body of Christ is important. You can utilize technology and your skill set the same way that a musician or worship leader uses the gift God gave them. It's an incredible opportunity to see the fruit of your hours of ministry when you can actually see a tangible transformation of someone's life changed forever.

I wanted to highlight the opportunity to reach people in a new way but also caution you that live streaming has its own set of challenges. I would recommend working on all of your video positions and team members before streaming live. That way your team is already comfortable with the routine before adding in the stress of a live broadcast. When live streaming, you should consider the following before starting or if you want to improve the experience.

AUDIO

To provide the best product you can, best practices would be to have a separate mix for the online audience. This is not always practical and can also be a limitation if qualified volunteers are scarce. One of the things I try to work with churches on is refining and making your live mix the best it can be. Often if you improve your live mix, it can improve your online mix as well. This is a good intermediate step while you work on funding and the volunteer base to complete a full audio position for the stream.

STREAM HOST

Once you begin streaming, you may want to have a host or a moderator to greet viewers online. They can take prayer requests, post sermon notes, and interact with the online audience instead of relying on them to just watch the service. You could also have an onscreen host that greets the viewers and speaks directly to them before service starts or after service ends. This is just a way to connect with them and make them feel part of the service even if it was through an online stream. Engaging with your audience is crucial in maintaining viewers. I also find it a good idea to encourage people to share the stream. You never know the reach you may have by your audience sharing to their group of friends.

MULTI-PLATFORM

We recommend streaming to multiple platforms for the best results. If you only stream to Facebook, you are limiting your audience. If you only stream to YouTube, you will capture a smaller audience than your potential. We recommend streaming with a paid service than can aggregate your stream and send it simultaneously to many platforms that you use—including streaming directly to your website. This also allows you to diversify your options in the event a site goes down or has a malfunction.

Keep in mind most social media platforms are free and you have no guarantee of quality of service so streaming to a provider where you can embed on your website is key.

Copyright

When streaming online, your services can get removed or have audio muted in the event of a copyright infringement claim. You also need to check with CCLI to ensure you have the proper streaming licenses for worship and music. As the church, we believe we should do things legally and that will require some license subscriptions. Also, any preservice music should be royalty-free and non-copyrighted.

Working Together

As with all the previous roles we talked about, the video team is no different. You have to work together with your Pastors, leaders, front-of-house, and with each other to have a successful ministry. This is such an important role today with the church as you can preserve sermons and services for generations to come. It is easy to get caught up in the equipment and get discouraged if you do not have a budget to do all the things we talked about.

Let me encourage you with this. Start with what you have. If you know the vision as we discussed, start working towards that vision a little at a time. You do not have to start with a full 3-4 camera system with a switcher and lower thirds. Start with one camera and master that. Be a good steward of what you do have and try to develop your team as you grow. Sometimes, it's possible to purchase an entire full video system and implement it but then overnight you have to grow your volunteer base.

Be faithful in what you are given to manage and steward and that includes your volunteers. The beauty of a video ministry is that it can grow with you. In addition to your team, you also will have to work with front-of-house to adjust lighting for video if this is new to your church as well as adjust the audio for video as well. It takes all members of the team working together to make the best, finished product possible.

~ KEY TAKEAWAY ~

**Define Your 5–10-Year Vision.
Be a Good Steward of Your
Equipment and Volunteers.**

CHAPTER 6

ENVIRONMENT ELEMENTS

I think the main goal or desire for a church service should be to eliminate as many distractions as possible so first-time guests feel comfortable while attending. The environmental elements and the people that make this a reality often are the ones that you never see. The environmental elements could be anything from the stage design to the lighting technician or even the backstage coordinator. We will highlight a few of these roles on the following pages.

TECHNICAL PRESENTATION

My wife should be writing this chapter as she has many more years of experience with this than I do. One of the things I have observed over the years is her feeling like what she does is not important. Let me start this chapter by saying, what you do matters. More importantly, YOU matter. I would say this is one of the most important roles in all of service production yet is also one of the most overlooked.

Pro Presenter has quickly become the defacto industry-standard software for most churches; though, you may also be using Easy Worship, Media Shout, or Power-Point among others. The software you use is not as important as what you are responsible for during a service.

The role of the Presentation Technician is to support the worship and teaching experience by operating presentation software with excellence and attention to detail, by displaying song lyrics, playing videos, showing images, and providing message-based note slides as needed. I have heard people say, "anyone can do that job" or "that's the easiest job in the booth." It takes a special person with a certain skill set to do this job with excellence and is an act of worship as well. I will never forget a service where my wife was running presentation, and nothing was going right that day. Lyrics were messed up, videos did not play correctly, and the communicator's sermon notes were inaccurate.

It is obvious to the congregation when something like that happens, as it is on all the screens throughout the church. She got to the point of literally crawling under the desk in the booth and crying in the middle of service. The type of person who is great at running presentations is generally the perfectionist whose attention to detail is high and who desires a mistake-free service. This is sometimes difficult to achieve and can be embarrassing and hard for the person with those qualities when mistakes happen.

So, let me start by saying, mistakes happen, you are still valued, and people will still be saved. You are more than a "button-pusher," not only is what you are doing an act of worship, but you are leading everyone on the platform as well as the congregation.

YOUR ROLE WITH THE STAGE COMMUNICATORS

People that are on stage for a service through the worship team, prayer, or sermon communicator all have many things that they must keep up with while on stage. When you run Technical Presentation, you are responsible for helping move the order of service along without them having to be distracted by things that you can help them with.

Timing is key in when to advance the slides for the worship team and how to advance the slides during the sermon. This can become an art in and of itself to be able to follow the worship team as they go back into a chorus or following a communicator that jumps to different scriptures out of order. Remember, the role you are playing is to complement what is happening on stage and help people follow along. If the worship team is introducing a new worship song, you are helping lead the entire congregation in learning that song and participating in worship. Sometimes it is necessary to meet with the worship leader before service to go over any song changes or any new songs. Using a program like Planning Center ahead of time can truly help in planning out the needs for the technical presentation role. The more detailed and more familiar you are with the service order, the better you will be able to execute your role.

As with many of the other positions that we have talked about, communication is the most important skill set when preparing for a service. The worship team relies on the words being correct and in the right order, and the congregation and newcomers will be referencing the screens for lyrics if they are unsure. If your schedule allows it, try to be at practice when the band practices so you can begin to learn the order and learn the song especially if it's a new song or new version. If that is not practical or possible, the worship leader should be able to share with you an audio version of the song they are planning on doing so you can familiarize yourself with those transitions and timings.

It also should go without saying to ensure pronunciation, capitalization, and spellings are correct. Again, the goal is to reduce distractions for those on stage and also those in the audience. Misspelled words can easily become a distraction. One of the best things you can do is to go over the order of service and check each slide for every transition before the service starts. If you are able to, also go through transitions with your audio and lighting personnel to make sure you are all on the same page and practice those transitions before the live event. In addition to checking all slides, all elements of a service should be tested including any videos or special items that will be shown in the service. If you get in the habit of testing the videos and slides before service, this will eliminate last-minute issues.

EXECUTION PROBLEMS

One of the biggest issues I hear from volunteers and staff alike is that they are not able to test slides because they do not get sermon notes from the Pastor or speaker until right before service. If you find yourself in this situation, go back and have a conversation about expectations and what is realistic.

Remember, if you are a Pastor, bringing those items at the last minute can cause stress, anxiety, and panic for your team. I understand sometimes it cannot be avoided, but if you try to set yourself a deadline and stick to it, the team and the service will run much smoother.

Another challenge may be that you are not able to get everything done on a Sunday morning. You can work on putting the presentation software on a laptop that someone can bring home to work on during the week or work with your IT provider to set up secured remote access for someone to get the presentations set up before the event ahead of time. If you can do that, then you could focus just on the sermon slides on a Sunday.

Communicating and figuring out what works for your team and organization is the main point. What works for one may not work for another but being open and honest about the process will instill trust and understanding. These are all things that can be done to try and set everyone up for the best success!

LIGHTING, STAGE DESIGN, AND ATMOSPHERE

The visual elements of service production are as much an important part as what you hear. Aside from the role of the producer in a service production setting, your lighting technician role will likely play the biggest part in making transitions go smoothly. Your visual stage design and lighting often go hand in hand so we will discuss both in this section.

It is becoming increasingly difficult to keep the attenion of this generation. With movies, concerts, TV shows, etc, our attention span seems to get shorter and shorter with each generation. One of the most popular apps right now is TikTok and most videos on there are under 3 minutes. Keeping the attention of people in this current society is an increasingly difficult challenge. I believe this is a prime example of being *in* the world, but not *of* it. We have to learn how to adapt and utilize technology to enhance the end goal of reaching people.

Creating an environment that is captivating to your audience and able to keep their attention is a tough job because in a church setting you also do not want it to be a distraction. We discussed your role in service production as helping your communicators on stage be able to perform their role with minimal distractions. Your job with stage design and lighting is also to not be distracting to the congregation.

As a creative person, it is easy to overproduce a lighting show without thinking about how distracting it has the potential to be. Your role in this is to always add to the overall production and not take away from it. As subjective as sound can be, stage and lighting design can also be just as subjective and hard to try and capture the vision of the Senior Pastor. I have a hard time articulating what I like to see from a design perspective and sometimes it is easier for me to see it than to try to explain to someone what I like. I find that many Pastors have the same struggle; they may not know how to say what they want to see and sometimes it's helpful to meet with them during the week to begin to learn what they like and don't like from a lighting and set design perspective. This should always be fluid and changing. Many times, you're going to change your set, your lay-out, your band positions, and sometimes it can help to see a visual of what other churches are doing.

Do not be afraid to have an open dialogue with your leadership team. It can be as informal as seeing something online and sending it to them to see if that is something they would like to implement. The vision and heart of where you are serving will be a running theme in this book. I realize, for some, your lighting may be switches on the wall or a set of a few par cans. No matter what you have at your disposal or what training you have, always remember you are in a position of servanthood to your volunteers and to your Pastor. Fulfilling the vision that God has given him for your church is your number one priority no matter what your church has for equipment.

I believe as technology and society continue to change; the church will have to continue to adapt to new ways of doing things. I want to be clear, technology in church should be complementary not the primary focus of a service. As your production team matures, you may add in components such as LED stage design, environmental projection, haze, smells, etc. All of these things can enhance and elevate the experience for a newcomer.

We have to remember that our target demographic is not the congregation at the church down the street. It is the couple that went to the club the night before, the college student that is studying for finals, the teenager who was abandoned by his parents, or the single mom trying to make ends meet.

Once you understand that technology is just a tool to reach those people, it's easier to embrace technology and use it just for its purpose, to attract and retain the attention of those you are trying to reach. Environmental and service production will be a forever changing part of ministry. Understanding it and keeping up with trends will always be a part of church service production.

~ KEY TAKEAWAY ~

Communicate with the Communicators.

CHAPTER 7

SERVICE COORDINATOR, PRODUCER, TEAM LEADER

Service Coordinator, Producer, Team Leader, or whatever title you give this position is not as important as understanding the role and responsibilities of this position. Depending on your team dynamic, the number of volunteers, and your team's skill level will determine the skill set needed to fill this role. I often see this position overlooked in small and large churches alike but having someone in place to lead and direct the service is crucial to minimize mistakes and help build up your team.

To be clear, the word "producer" can have a negative connotation for some people that do not like the feeling that a church service is a "production" and I understand that sentiment. However, it is the closest word I can think of to describe what the person's responsibilities would be. It is not the title that matters but the *why* as we described in Chapter 1.

THE IDEAL CANDIDATES

Many of the characteristics of a producer will be the same no matter the size of your team but can be challenging if you have a much smaller church or volunteer team. So, I am going to break down the ideal candidate into two categories and describe each. This is a general idea of what your ideal person may look like when you are thinking of having a producer role for your church but needs to be adjusted to fit your culture and team dynamic.

As you are identifying and building your service production team, you may not be able to start with a producer or may only have one type of personality on your team. I will explain the different types. Unless you have someone that fills both roles, it could also be split into two different positions such as a producer and a technical producer. Both of these personalities are crucial to the team for different reasons.

THE MOTIVATOR – IDEAL FOR LARGER CHURCHES AND LARGER TEAMS

If your team is rather large and technically proficient, you may be able to have a producer that has the personality of a motivator. Generally, this works well if you have very seasoned volunteers or paid technical staff. Your producer role, in this case, is to coordinate transitions between teams during a service and motivate the team to excellence.

This person would not necessarily have to be as technical since your team is proficient in the execution of their positions. This could also be a staff Pastor, but I do caution that this person should be in the booth and part of the service production team and not have shared or other responsibilities. As a motivator personality, you need to be alongside your team and build those relationships with your volunteers and that needs to be part of your responsibility and your focus during the service.

Some qualities and responsibilities of a Motivator

- Help define, execute and teach the overall vision and purpose
- Set goals for the team
- Empower and trust the volunteers
- Call out transitions and make sure everyone is aware of changes
- Be the point of contact for staff to communicate changes or adjustments
- Be able to handle conflict and resolve matters quickly
- Be approachable and personable
- Be a great listener and teacher
- Be able to coach, correct, teach, and listen

This person is generally more outgoing, a people person, and typically a dominant or driven personality that is very goal-oriented. They are not always the most technical and sometimes you may need a more technical producer.

THE TECHNICIAN – SMALLER TEAMS OR SOMEONE WITH MORE OF AN INTROVERTED PERSONALITY

Most of the time, people who volunteer in service production love to be behind the scenes and many have a more introverted personality. This is crucial in making sure you have the right people in the right positions. If you give someone who is not naturally a motivator, the same responsibilities as a motivator, they typically will struggle in this area if you make them handle conflict or they may have anxiety in trying to lead a team when that is not natural to them. It can be taught over time, but you should identify these personality types early before asking someone to fill this role that could be outside his or her comfort zone.

A great team-building exercise is to have your team do a DISC profile of some sort so you can see how they are naturally wired. If you have someone on your team that is more technical, they could be considered a Technical Producer. If you have someone that is highly technical, they can fill this role and you can have less skilled volunteers fill the positions for service knowing your technical producer can troubleshoot problems. This person generally learns very fast and if you have someone that is a natural-born troubleshooter, these are the qualities and responsibilities they may have:

- Learn all service production positions

- Learn how the systems work together to know how to fix issues

- Take over and help troubleshoot issues as they arise for each position

- Be a backup to help the team when they experience a technical failure

- Responsible for maintenance and processes

- Able to jump in and run any position as needed

Often these personalities are great with technology but do not have the skill set or comfort level to handle some of the duties of a motivator. Finding the right person to fit the right role will help your team grow and help create the culture that fits your team and your organization.

THE TECHNICAL MOTIVATOR

In very rare circumstances, you find someone that has the qualities of both a motivator and a technician. This is usually common for people that work or have worked in production environments before, or have technical experience as well as leadership qualities. If you have identified people on your team, that have these qualities, begin investing in them now, as they are very rare and very valuable to the growth and culture of your team.

I believe both natural personality types mentioned above can grow and learn to ultimately be able to fulfill the role of a Technical Motivator but understand that each person is different in how they learn and how quickly they grow. A natural motivator will need to slow down and learn every position, how to troubleshoot and how to fix things quickly.

All of those are learned skills and also help them to be better leaders of the team because they truly understand how to work in each position. I think this is important when you are the leader to be able to put yourself in the shoes of those you are leading. Often churches have the Worship Pastor or Lead Pastor try to fill the role of leading the production team. I recommend not to do that without also having a producer position as well. As I stated, you need someone in the booth, working alongside your team to understand the full dynamic of what goes into a successful service. This will help in the long run to provide a balance and understanding between staff and the service production volunteers to better understand one another. Having someone who can deal with conflict and also understand the intricacies of multiple systems is invaluable to your service production team.

OTHER RESPONSIBILITIES

Your producer should lead by example and be one of the first ones there for service to welcome your staff and volunteers. It is important to check on each team member at the start of each service and make sure they are in a posture ready to serve. Having one person show up on your team for a service that is having a bad day or having an attitude can affect the entire morale of the team.

As the leader, you should have the relationship and awareness if someone may need to reach out or have a conversation. Try to make it a priority to talk to each team member on a personal level and build that relationship before diving right into the order of service or role responsibilities. Making sure your team is ready to serve is just as important as them knowing the details of a service. Always remember the *why*.

TECHNICAL RUN THROUGH

Many churches have multiple services on a weekend so having a technical run-through before your first service of the weekend is very important. If you have a night of worship or a single service, the same run-through should apply. As the leader, make sure your team is in place early enough to go through an entire technical run-through. Typically, this will be after soundcheck but before the pre-service meeting. It is during this time that you are checking everything from a technical perspective.

Make sure all slides for all songs are in the correct order and your volunteer is familiar with the songs. Practice all transitions between videos and slides and test audio. If live-streaming, test the stream so you know you are ready to go once service starts. This is the time when you should change batteries in wireless microphones and make sure every microphone is tested through the system including any speaker microphones. Try to catch as many mistakes as you can here to try and eliminate as many as you can for service.

Practicing those transitions will allow everyone on your team to know the ending of any videos and know the cues they need to know before the service begins.

PRE-SERVICE

Before each service, you should hold a pre-service meeting to discuss any last-minute changes, take notes, and allow your team to ask any questions for clarity. The more you communicate on the front-end, the smoother your service will flow.

I recommend you meet with your technical team, worship team, Lead Pastor representative, and anyone that will have a role in making your service a success. If you have something like communion, baptism, or graduation, you may want to have the lead usher or guest services team help in coordinating any last-minute issues.

You must plan for this meeting and make it a part of your volunteers' schedule. If you do not, it will always be put off and not prioritized. Make sure your team is there early enough to get service preparation done so you are able to attend and focus on this meeting.

We recommend the following be covered to provide clarity to the team:

- Meet for approximately 5 minutes, 15-20 minutes before service

- Go through the order of service

- Highlight sermon title or theme

- Open the floor to questions for clarity

- Pray over the service and the team

Try to start these meetings on time and end them on time in case you come across any changes that need to be made with your technical team. If any changes are communicated, make sure your team prioritizes those changes to ensure they are all updated before service begins.

SERVICE DEBRIEF

Just as important as the pre-service meeting is your service debrief. If you have multiple services, I recommend doing one of these after the first service to make sure any adjustments are made quickly. This also allows you to praise your team for the things that went well and make adjustments where needed. I would have a representative from the worship team as well as any notes from the Lead Pastor and your technical team there to go through anything that needs to change. You can also do this in the sound booth to keep everyone close between services if you have multiple services.

I recommend starting this meeting by praising your team for a job well done and then coaching them in any areas that need improvement. This is a key distinction that you coach, not correct. Coaching your team rather than correcting your team shows respect and honor to that person.

Mistakes will happen, equipment will fail, and things will go wrong. Being able to adapt in the moment and learn how to improve in those times will make your entire team better.

~ KEY TAKEAWAY ~

Over-Communicate and be Intentional!

CHAPTER 8

ADMINISTRATION, MAINTENANCE, BUDGETS AND VENDORS

Your production team can only be as good as the administrative team you have behind it. Understanding all aspects of the ministry you serve and the volunteers you lead can be a challenge, especially if you are a technical person—administration may come hard for you. Administration and being able to plan ahead will help you mold and shape your team and leadership's vision.

I have seen churches time and again invest thousands of dollars into an AVL system thinking it is a one-time investment and not understanding the overall maintenance and budget that it will take to properly maintain the system. The total cost of ownership should be taken into consideration when deciding on budget and maintenance schedules. In this chapter, we are going to look at some ways to help you plan for budgets and maintenance schedules for your AVL system.

BUDGETS - KNOW YOUR CULTURE

Before we break down budget ideas for full systems and maintenance, you should know the culture of the organization you are a part of. What does your church think about debt? Do they have opposition to leasing equipment? Is the preferred method to pay cash? What kind of expectations do they have for ongoing expenses? Do they operate from capital expenditures or operating expenditures?

Knowing the answer to these questions will help you plan your system and budget effectively. If you have never had this conversation with your leadership team, you should talk this out together to determine the best way to approach coming up with a budget. Nothing can be more frustrating for someone over service production than to spend hours putting together a system or budget only to find out later you are so far apart from the leadership's expectations.

My biggest word of advice here is to not assume and guess at this. Having an open and honest conversation about budgets and expectations is healthy and will save time and frustration if you discuss this on the front end. It is also a good idea to find out from other churches that match your demographic what they have spent and what they typically budget. This will sometimes help set realistic expectations especially if your team is not aware of the true cost of high-end equipment. If I were to ask three different people to go and purchase a vehicle for me, it is very likely I would get back three different options. One may have brought me an SUV, one could have brought a Sedan, and one a sports car. Without finding out what the use of the vehicle was going to be and then narrowing that down to how much I wanted to spend, it does not allow you enough information to make an informed decision.

The same applies when you are working on a service production budget. If you are tasked to work on a budget to renovate your AVL system, it will be very inefficient and almost impossible to do without establishing some basic parameters. This is a conversation you and your leadership should have before starting down that path. While these are not all-inclusive, these are some basic questions I would ask for trying to develop a budget. These questions are helpful when designing a system budget or a yearly operating budget as well.

1. What is the total budget the church or organization feels comfortable with spending?

2. What specifically are we trying to accomplish and what are the non-negotiables? For instance, your leadership team might want your front-line singers all on wireless microphones because they want the stage look to be clean. Another example would be the online audience etc. You need to get as specific as possible, so you can break down what you must have to fulfill the vision and goal.

3. Is lease-to-purchase an option or are you going to pay cash for everything?

4. What is the vision for the growth of the organization? If you put in a system now that the main auditorium outgrows, can it be repurposed for a youth/kid's system in the future?

5. What equipment can be reused instead of replacing everything? This is important because it shows you want to be a good steward of the church's money. You are trying to extend the life of the equipment and reuse items when necessary.

6. What is the disaster plan in the event something does not work for a service? For instance, if you go to a digital soundboard, what happens if it will not boot up one Sunday? Do you have a backup plan for if/when that happens? This may be something you want to consider when choos-

ing soundboards. You can standardize your consoles in the youth/kid's room, so you have spares in the event of a failure.

7. Will the chosen equipment be able to be run by volunteers or will it require paid professionals? This is an important question if you are buying a much larger system, as it can get complicated very quickly for a volunteer to run.

8. Identify who needs to be involved in the decision process. I cannot stress how important this is. The worship leader to the finance director, may all need to be involved in the process. Identify who on your team will make up that group and make sure you communicate clearly.

This is not an exhaustive list of questions but should at least be discussed when identifying and knowing the culture of your organization. Having these questions answered at the beginning of the budget process will help you know how to plan for and execute your budget and help fulfill the ministry's vision.

WHAT NUMBERS DO I USE?

We often get asked how much a church should spend on an AVL budget for a new construction project. While no exact formula is scientific, we do find that 10-20% of the total cost of a building project would provide adequate systems. This can vary based on style of worship, traditional or contemporary services, LED vs projectors, etc. But if you plan 10-20% you should have an adequate amount to spend to properly outfit the building with appropriate systems. For example, if you were to build a $1,000,000 building, you could plan for around 15% ($150,000) for a moderate system to be put in.

The next logical question we get asked is, what should we spend on our AVL budget annually? This varies greatly from church to church but typically for maintenance alone, we find a budget of 10% of your system cost should be allocated to maintain that system every year.

So, in our above example, you could budget $15,000/ year to maintain that system and keep it in proper working condition. That would include things like projector bulbs, amplifier repair, speaker repair, light bulbs, etc.—basically, things to maintain the system. In addition to that number, you would also budget things like batteries, upgrades, other purchases or labor that would not necessarily be maintenance. So this, would be in addition to your maintenance budget.

Budgets are not one size fits all and it generally depends on many factors, however the above should provide you with a good starting point when you are trying to create something that works for you and your team.

OTHER BUDGET CONSIDERATIONS

EMERGENCY FUND

The inevitable is going to happen and you should make it a priority to plan for the inevitable. You do not want your failure to plan to turn into an all-out emergency. As you are working with your leadership team, you should develop an emergency fund for your AVL systems that will help cover the cost if a key piece of equipment fails. These may be items like a central video switcher, light board, single projector, presentation computer, or digital soundboard. Any piece of equipment that cannot be easily replaced is a core system of the organization.

For instance, if you only had a single camera for live streaming, that would be considered a core piece of equipment. If you had a 4 camera system for your live stream, you could lose a camera and still operate. You could not lose a camera switcher and easily operate, so in this case, your switcher would be considered essential. Identifying the gear that you are unable to easily operate a service without, will help you determine how much money to put aside in your emergency fund.

SINKING FUND

In the real estate world, a sinking fund is money that you put aside for a specific purpose to replace big-ticket items such as a roof. A roof on a commercial building needs to be changed every 20-30 years so instead of a huge expense happening all at once, they put money aside each month to have the available cash when the repair is needed.

The same should apply to your budget for AVL systems. Many factors go into this determination, but I believe a system should be fully replaced every 10-15 years, at the most. If you want to replace your audio system every 15 years, figure out what that budget will be, and then set aside that money on a monthly or yearly basis for 15 years, so you have the cash to pay for it when that time comes.

If you plan this out, you are not in a crisis mode to replace something and have to find a way to pay for it. Also, if you are able to get another few years out of the system, you can still replace it at any given point without it being an emergency and it will be paid for in cash.

VENDORS AND PARTNERSHIPS

It has become common practice and expected to source equipment and technology through online websites and box houses. I use them all the time and have become accustomed to 2nd-day shipping or next-day delivery. These companies have their place but do not overlook the value of having a local consultant whom you can meet with and strategize about your goals and vision. It is almost impossible for a church to keep up with how fast technology is changing and how quickly things become outdated. Partnering with a vendor you can trust gives you a huge advantage of not wasting money or spending funds unwisely.

Sometimes in leadership, we put unrealistic expectations on staff or volunteers to advise us on what we need to do to solve a problem or what equipment we need to buy and we do not consult an expert that can give us more insight. One of the benefits of working with a vendor partner is that they have seen many other installations, configurations, and churches. They have knowledge that you can utilize to help make the best decision. You do need to find a vendor that you trust and one that aligns with your vision and understands your budget constraints. Having these relationships can also help if a piece of equipment fails or you need help setting up new equipment. When you buy online, you do not get the personal help and relationship from someone as when you buy from a local vendor. I am not saying that you should never buy technology online, but leverage your local contacts to help you make long-term decisions that will help fulfill your vision.

~ KEY TAKEAWAY ~

Plan Your Budget, Budget Your Plan.

CHAPTER 9

CHANGING THE CULTURE

Remember my *why*? I am not the most qualified to write this book, but I know that many people involved in church service production struggle with acceptance, hurts, struggles, leadership, and depression. If you are involved in ministry and have never felt this way, please read this chapter carefully as I do not want to tarnish or blemish anyone in any way.

If you are a Pastor, I ask you to read this and understand the heart of people that may be currently serving on your team. If you are a volunteer and have ever felt some of the ways described in the next few pages, know that you are not alone and you can find fulfillment and acceptance. If you have never felt this way before, someone around you probably has.

I pray this specifically will be eye-opening and helpful to people that feel similar things or help leaders identify things they want to avoid. If nothing else, I hope it raises awareness for you to see your fellow volunteers with compassion.

In preparation for writing this book, I posted a question to a few social media groups I am involved in that have mostly people involved in church service production in one way or another. The results and answers I received shocked me. In under 30 minutes, I received over 200 responses. The answers to this one question changed the entire book to what you are reading today.

The question I asked was: What is the number one struggle you have in leading or volunteering in church service production?

The answers I received to that question took me by surprise honestly. Below are excerpts I received from many different people when asked that question.

> "Keeping up with skills and training others, investing in people's lives while caring for your own life —paid or unpaid, it is a lot. The payoff can be immense if your whole team's hearts are in the right place."

"Me becoming bitter...The lack of genuine care from those who are actually staff."

"It's extremely difficult when you are an unpaid servant. Especially when you serve in a role that is vital (like sound engineer). Then people who don't honestly understand come at you with suggestions/criticism and they have not one time ever asked you how you are doing. Or even said here take your family out for supper on me because we know how much time you have put in here."

"Always "working" and not building relationships. It was the precursor to me leaving a previous church I served at for over 10 years when I realized I really only knew tech and worship team people."

"Managing big personalities with sometimes competing ideas."

"Remembering that I need breaks from time to time and that I'm only human and only one person."

"Mean, rude people."

"Not being overbearing—I often am running house and stream on my own, and really need my other person to just sort of do what I tell them. I am open to new ideas, but not if it's coming from someone who hasn't shown commitment. I'm finding that I stifle my constructive comments because I'm desperate for a warm body to help."

"Not being able to minister the way God desires us to."

"Finding time to rest, take breaks, take care of myself. And find my own time to connect with Jesus away from the church setting."

"Feeling like it's a task rather than an act of worship."

"Inorganization and unpreparedness."

"Leadership or lack of leadership to better put it."

"Dealing with other volunteers that don't put in any amount of the real effort needed to handle this role and responsibilities."

"A "it's good enough." Or "they did their best" mentality. Or lack of respect and reverence for the platform in general."

"Building relationships, leading by example, consistency, accountability, setting realistic expectations, not being afraid to upset people, and lots of grace while having difficult conversations."

"Feeling responsible for everything and not having a break from doing."

"Getting volunteers and trying to teach our current volunteers to pay attention to the details during the service."

"Poor communication."

"Working around bad arrangements."

"Cultural issues."

"Other volunteers not showing up and not letting anyone know about it. That and worship team leaders waiting till the last minute to let us know the song list and service schedule. 20 minutes before the start of service is at least 3 days too late."

"Micromanagement."

"Getting scriptures/songs or wanting something special last minute. By last minute I mean 10 mins or less before service starts."

"Personality/power struggles."

"The Pastor's criticism of the volunteer's ability."

"Probably that most Pastors think they know better than the guy who has the engineering degree and 25 years of experience... It's an ego trip. I've seen it time and time again. Now, in their defense, I'm not talking about a Pastor requesting a 90db max, or more in the monitors. I'm talking about the guys who think they need to micro-manage the sound guy like the office personnel. They think they know the best place to mount speakers, to place wedges, how to mix drums, etc. It's a "control thang" from a controlling personality."

"To be completely honest. Trusting people in the church. About to turn fifty-nine, been hurt by many people in churches over the past. Victim of vicious lies, deception, greed, control and deception. Of course, I am speaking past tense, I know I am supposed to forgive and forget. When the wounding is deep so are the scars. I don't serve to serve people, I serve to serve God. There are a lot of so-called believers with an agenda that best serves themselves and their goals. Don't worry I am working on it."

"Honestly, and this is just me on a personal level in my professional life and my time as unpaid staff. I need to learn to set boundaries. That's the hardest part of boundaries in terms of when to take time for me and a break. I always am working myself to death (out of passion, not workaholic)."

"Trying to ensure that my volunteers' walk with God is not affected by their service on my team while being understaffed."

"Being seen as just the Audio Engineer and not a member of the church. I often feel like a third wheel sitting in the booth or an afterthought. It's odd to explain."

"I also struggle with countless hours of volunteering and watching other people get paid. We're often there before people arrive and after people leave. We spend countless hours preparing our stages for each service and have people criticize our work."

"The new Director/Pastor trusting the well-seasoned volunteers to know their craft."

"Being referred to as "just one of the volunteers" in numerous settings—despite a master's in engineering, being qualified in numerous disciplines (many paid for me to better support my voluntary work). I have come across a slight arrogance many times (not in my current church I hasten to add) from those who work full-time for a church or charity and somehow seem to believe they are the only ones who really understand <insert topic X>. As was excellently described above—I'm not here to serve an earthly master so shrug it off and get on with the job."

"From a volunteer perspective: putting in years of work, way over and above other volunteers' hours and work output, but not being valued by leadership."

"Having my hands tied due to budgetary restrictions."

"Others on the team not understanding what it takes to make service production happen with care for quality (equipment, manpower, skill, attention to detail, communication, intentionality, etc) and equating those things to "trying to entertain.""

"Getting someone, anyone who wants to learn how to be "the sound guy" and help out. I have no one."

"The "we need it now" attitude and micromanagement."

IT'S ABOUT RELATIONSHIPS

I hope those quotes resonated with you on some level. If you are a volunteer or paid staff and feel that way, I am sorry. If you are a Pastor or in a leadership position, be intentional with your volunteers and get to know them. I truly do not believe anyone intentionally makes people feel this way. I just think church service production is sometimes seen as an afterthought until something goes wrong. Some of the most instrumental people to pull off a weekend service sit in the box in the back of the room and push buttons, work years, and are never really known. It's hard to read all of those different people's stories and not want to help. I hope in writing this book I have helped at least one person out there.

"You cannot outsource or delegate your intentionality when it comes to relationships."

So, I am asking you to help change the culture in church service production circles. We all need to be more intentional and understanding of the volunteers and relationships around us. No matter where you are in your production journey, I hope you got something useful out of these words. My intention and prayer is that as a community, we begin to change the culture of our teams one person at a time, one church at a time, and one ministry at a time.

After reading some of these responses, go back and re-read Chapter 1—Define Your *Why*, and think about the people on your production team. Do any of them feel the way these others do?

~ KEY TAKEAWAY ~

Change The Culture.

ABOUT THE AUTHOR

Paul Mancuso is the President and CEO of Vital Integrators based out of Lafayette, LA. Vital Integrators is one of under 40 companies in the United States to have earned the CompTIA Security Trustmark+ and the only company in the state of Louisiana to have received this certification. Vital knows and understands ministry, Cyber Security, AVL systems and specializes in integrating them all together to work seamlessly. Vital provides premium IT support for businesses and nonprofits across the Gulf Coast and the United States. At Vital they always start with security. Your systems need to be protected to function at peak performance. Vital integrates and maintains all your VITAL (Video, IT, Audio, and Lighting) systems together, with a unique focus on cybersecurity and ease of use. Vital Integrators currently employs 10 staff members and has customers along the Gulf Coast from Texas to Florida.

Paul has a unique perspective and understanding of the IT industry as a Managed Service Provider but also installs and designs audio, video, and lighting systems for churches and businesses that have a strong desire to integrate those systems around a core IT infrastructure with a cybersecurity focus. He desires to provide a personal and accurate service to clients by helping both businesses and end-users fully utilize technology to enhance day-to-day operations. As a Managed Service Provider, Vital Integrators focuses on putting client security first with a custom security and productivity platform. Paul has a passion for helping others using technology. His mission in business, as in life, is to empower people to become their very best. And when people and organizations take advantage of the ever-changing landscape of technology, with increased efficiency and cost-saving measures, they can't help but find themselves better.

Clients rely heavily upon Vital Integrators' problem-solving skills, which are oftentimes superior because of their composite experience in such a wide range of fields. Because Paul possesses such an extensive scope of knowledge in various areas of technology, he is often able to make recommendations for using technology more to the organization's advantage and can assist in developing new systems when the need arises. Paul is passionate about the fast-paced changes in the IT world. "I love the industry because you can never stop learning. If you stop learning, your career is effectively over." Paul is extremely motivated by the challenge of helping to redirect the course of an organization through the proper use of technology, and he takes great satisfaction in helping them save money in the process.

In addition to all the good he brings to the IT aspects of organizations, Paul and his wife, Misty, have been married for nearly 20 years, and have two sons Landon and Greyson. Paul was raised in church from a very early age and having a heart for the house of God is a value he is working to instill in his children as well. It does not require spending very much time in Paul's presence before you realize that God and people matter the most to him. He never passes up the opportunity to help others, and his wife and children mean the world to him. He selflessly goes out of his way to serve those in need, and because of his heart for others, the integrity with which he conducts every aspect of his life, and the wealth of knowledge and experience he brings to the table, any organization will be privileged to partner with him in their endeavors.